Gjallarhorn

Gjallarhorn:
Journal of Germanic Esotericism

By

Agony's Point Press

© Copyright Agony's Point Press
agonyspoint.substack.com

ISBN: 9798883451484

Gjallarhorn

Raventongue: Introduction

With many persons flooding into a reborn Germanic Esotericism via the release of SHADOWS OVER GERMANIA, *Gjallarhorn Journal* was launched in an attempt to provide background information on that which is hidden, or less accented on this subject. For one manner of attractiveness that Draugrism presents to its adherents is that *it is not contrived* and *it is not fabricated,* unlike other adjacent practices claiming an indigenous European pedigree. In this, Draugrism produces authentic spirituality that is connected to the blood. To accompany this experience is the necessary folklore, legends and mysteries that connect us to the ancient past, and sometimes provide insight into the present. Whereas the Draugr Cult volumes are

Gjallarhorn

concentrated in esoteric teachings as related to the magickal current, *Gjallarhorn* adds supplementary information that add to the mythic accord in question.

Draugr Cult by contrast excels in this area, synthesizing the ancient and the modern, as to presence the forces of the North in a practical way — here in our current year of

Germanic Esotericism is largely understudied, and exists in a fragmented manner, often without real explanation born from a personal striving and direct experience(s) with the forces or nature. The

2024 a.y.p.s.

For our first issue we have selected several subjects of pertinence. All however are controversial in their own right, examining the reality of our magickal subject

Gjallarhorn

without the hindrance of limitation. We in the Draugr Cult believe this to be a terrible folly: to twist and distort that which one doesn't believe is congruent with their moral choices. The superior option is to apply intelligence to these instances and survey what comes from rational discussion. In this way, our journal serves as an arena to educate, reveal and analyze the setting of which our occult weltanschauung envisages the cosmos.

For far too long the least qualified minds have been applied to this general subject and the instantaneous result of Gjallarhorn is the imperative to arrest these thought forms so spun into the very fabric of Odinism. As this mythic world in which we can see and access regularly is neither kind nor forgiving, and here marks the *end* of such profuse intimations. Here marks the *conclusion* of their error.

Therefore we declare: "öffnen und waschsen Wodanaz" — let us throw open the black gate of Mordor and charge with furious violence towards these difficult literary topics unafraid of the outcome. The world is still very much "in the dark" about Germanic Esotericism, and we are here to provide the hideous illumination that crackles terrible laughter from the funeral pyre.

Gjallarhorn

Sumbel:
On Worship

Every now and again in Pagan subcultures, the quandary of justification for the worship of the divinities envisaged by our ancestors is postulated. The impetus for this investigation is entirely located in the momentum of changed or changing ethics and the morality that has been embodied by the epochs beyond the ubiquitously indigenous faith. While the analysis of this subject is worthy of its own article, let us conclude by moving forward and launching from the precipice that *we do not live in those times, not any longer*. Naturally, micro-societies have been built, in which, inside of their perimeters, a strong resurgent atavism or anachronism tends to occur, and this is why these *tribes* are gathered in the first place: so that persons might explore the full width of the time out of mind to which they seek.

But these make up a minority of the heathen dedicants that populate the globe today. For the most, they tend to live mentally, emotionally and behaviorally within our time period, even if they are informed by the past. And this is precisely where the conundrum arises. The question is asked then: are these divine forces, which have been characterized as such, *worthy* of our devotion, our rites, our life force and our mind's attention? Are they worthy of our passing this along to our future generations? Are they worthy of all these things, *even though, the times of olde have passed,* and with them, the customs so often associated with these beings? Can therefore a time-displaced archaic force find new or old or restored function... today?

One of the most time honored functions of mythology and folklore is to communicate societal expectations to the listener or reader or experiencer. It begins from divine example and trickles down to the human adventure, with all the variables of life accompanying. But if these tales, specifically those from the Germanic antiquity, are heavily characterized by customs, rites, patterns and deeds which would be considered entirely outmoded and even criminalized today, then where does the burning bridge from the ancient past to the modern world lead, other than to doom?

One could rationalize these things, as they should, but it is never examined how popular new religious movements such as Asatruar Kindreds will pay homage to Þórr, while collected within these exclusive circles, but call

Gjallarhorn

upon the police when confronted with an accostive gang, or an enemy. Is there an explanation as to why Odinists place their entire mind/body/soul into the hands of the Allfather, but not propitiate him with ghastly human sacrifices, and do not mirror his insatiable sexual perversity? Do they even know about that? If Yngwi-Freyr is your lord of joy, do you send your friends to threaten your love interests with boils and pox if they deny you?

Even in the most brutal of micro-societies, at least in the west, it's hard to imagine that anyone would do these things on a regular basis. Meanwhile they do tend to occur but most often *not* within the heathen sphere. If they were customary at one point, they aren't any longer, and there are now punitive consequences for these actions. Norse Mythology,

while being very expansive and rich in detail, is also redolent of a different time — the time to which these customs would have been considered commonplace. And yet they are codified still, locked indeed, into the archetypes therein. Óðinn will never stop being a savage womanizer, inspiring frenzy and bloodshed on the battlefield, stoking men and women's passions to the boiling point of sometimes lethal result. Loki will never stop being a murderer. Thor can not be reimagined into an archetype of universal, interracial-peace.

One could think that the Palestinians have undertaken the worship of Odin, with the sexualized violence harnessed as a weapon, and that the Israelis have begun to venerate Thor, marching forward with genocide in their eyes. These things still occur, but it appears that

Gjallarhorn

the civilizing elements of Christendom have surgically removed the functions of the Nordic Gods from our lives — or so it seems.

The lives of civilians tend to be less dramatic in terms of lethality today, and our range of behavioral mobility may be curtailed, but this must be seen within the eye of the beholder. The United States Military could effectively flatten *both* Israel and Palestine in a matter of hours using many possible strategies for the choosing. Therefore civilization in no way removes efficiency from a people, it just marshals compliance — and that compliance translates to power on the global, international scale. It conditions a populace through an insidious examples-based learning, oftentimes resolving 90% of the Dark-Age problems

without a sword being drawn. That is power.

That is Odinic.

Our agency to choose brutality is not limited, only *redirected.* In that, how many days in the west continue onward *without* the express knowledge of black operations occurring, which would if known, ultimately press the pause and rewind, fast forward and play buttons on our society without any measure of order? And this is what a trained eye can detect: forward looking. It is for these reasons and many more why the Draugr Cult does not see the absence of the Gods on our side, but the opposite. What was set down in the past belongs to that time and to those people. We keep them alive in our study and memory because they have the capability to offer insight into the present age.

Gjallarhorn

If there is one key characteristic that should be remembered about the Draugr Cult, it is that it knows which time period it belongs to currently.

Draugrism is a strain of Wamphyrism — a Germanic strain — and two things should be seen within the lens of this discussion about that praxis. Firstly, that it brings with it the fully operational theory of the Undead state *intact.* With this comes the perspective of: the present timeline as the only thing that is real. While the past has occurred already, it only ever happened *in the present* when it did. Now it is only a memory. The future is a postulation that will only happen once again: *in the present*. All three are important for operative esotericism, but there is only one that takes primacy. Which is truly the center most reason why we as the Draugr Cult have and are continuing to write about these subjects. We believe that within the available scope of modules orbiting Germanic Esotericism, we understand only our emanations as functional *today*. Many areas of similar or overlapping subjects suffer critically from a lack of effective esoteric technique — the Draugr does not. Nor does the Germanic Wamphyr regard our current epoch as unfavorable, in any way. Our reality is simply what it is. By choosing to accept its parameters as the frame from which one can function, and embracing it for all that it is, we see very clearly the footsteps of the Gods in our history well into the ages long since the Germanic past.

The ineffective, unstrategic anachronist, which is subject to even *considering* the reality of a operation of such savage times-past to be palpable today, is a fool, a patsy for a third world country, or both. If that's your destiny, and you have to fulfill it, basking in spirit of ancient barbarism, know now that our modern world is far more brutal and savage that whatever emotional dream you hold of the Iron Age. Our weapons are far more devastating, and our sciences produce mega-death. Our black arts are far more sinister than your trelldoms myriad. For our wounds simply *do not heal* when they are dealt. And while the ones you carve may be felt for a moment, the Draugr know how to extend that torment into a lifetime.

Gjallarhorn

The Rape of Rindr

In today's Heathen circles, the literacy of the mythos is beyond poor. To even suggest a scholastic destitution would be generous, as there has been, since as long back as can be understood, a nebulous hole from which random belief springs in terms of these matters. It happens that people tend to learn best through oral transmission — and to this we would say *great*, only, when this is the situation at hand, what is then discussed is what is ultimately transmitted.

In the Germanic Antiquity, these myths were recorded in entertaining formats of

Gjallarhorn

the time, many of which were clearly suggesting that they were to be performed, with actors and stanzas for each to say. Though in modern times with advanced technology and the development of the entertainment industry into the preferred mediums, what is considered to be *entertaining* has changed significantly. The proven and most effective manner of transmission however is within an intimate setting, between a small group of people, where one or several persons are entrusted with an esteemed or working knowledge of the legends and folklore.

Where this tends to fall short is when those whom this is bestowed upon heavily filters *what* is being said. And to this, much has been twisted to fit extremely focused agendas, and rarely ever is a clear, encyclopedic frame of reference used for this surefire method. In its place, a selective series of characterizations molded to paint a model of the Germanic divine in the image of the storyteller. The error is greater than one realizes, when such a vested interest is applied to this transmission.

The error is that the listener *does not apprehend* the reality of the entity. In the case of Óðinn, this is a most-egregious injustice. For the Allfather was called Yggr ("The Terrible One") for a reason. It was not just a *fun* or *scary* designation. It was deathly serious. None more so in the scope of recent times embodies this kenning than the tale of the *Rape of Rindr*, which retelling has been indeed barred from many heathen circles, often on the assumption that it is *Christian influence*, intended to serve as *conversion propaganda* of the time.

Gjallarhorn

It was not. At least not entirely. Though, much here is subject to speculation.

The tale unfolds in this manner. Balder the bright god, most beautiful of Asgard and son of Odin was the center of a contest: the demonstration that *nothing* could harm him. The host of the heavens threw every manner of weaponry at him, and he was therewith unharmed in the aftermath. Balder had only one weakness: mistletoe. When it was observed that Balder was invulnerable, Loki changed his shape into an old woman and approached the former's mother Frigg, wife of Odin, as asked her to explain why her son was invulnerable to all things. Frigg told Loki, while he was in disguise, that she had made all things swear not to harm Balder, except for a single plant that grew eastward, simply because it was too young to cause harm, in her estimation.

Loki then traveled to where it grew, most likely near Jotunheim, as that is eastward, and purloined a twig. He returned to the assembly on a night where this custom was being done and asked Hoðr, the blind god, to give Balder the honor of partaking in the demonstration. Hoðr explained that he was blind, and could not see where Balder was standing, to which Loki explained to him, that he would *guide his hand*. Hoðr then took the twig and threw it at Balder, to which it pierced him, unlike any other substance in the nine worlds, and he fell dead.

Balder entered Hel, and in an attempt to rescue him from the underworld, Hermoðr, his brother, rode the demon horse Sleipnir to the abode of the death goddess, and begged for his release. Hel agreed that if all souls in the nine worlds

Gjallarhorn

would weep for Balder's return, she would release him from the clutches of death. Upon return he explained this to the assembly of the Aesir, to which the campaign to weep for Balder began to form. However, Loki once more changed his shape into that of an old hag named Þokk, and vowed that she would not weep for Balder. This sealed his doom.

As a result of this and also a dramatic incident recorded in the *Lokasenna*, the most famous and well-crafted flyting poem of the antiquity, Loki's machinations were uncovered. Balder's brother Vali first killed Hoðr, and Loki was chased into the cave of Gnipa. From here there are various accounts of what happened but what appears to be the case when they are all examined is that Vali then transformed into a wolf, killed Loki's son Nari or Narfi, and then

disemboweled him, to which Loki was then bound in the entrails of his own child, to wait imprisoned until the day of Ragnarok, while a serpent drips venom onto his face to torture him, and as his consort Sigyn attempts to catch most of the venom in a receptacle, but when she empties the bowl or dish, venom would reach his face, and thus Loki's torment in his subterranean lair is why earthquakes would occur.

What is rarely spoken about, is what occurred *between* the death of Balder, and the binding of Loki. This regards the Rape of Rindr, and the birth of Vali.

After proper consultations and scheming had occurred, Allfather Odin traveled to the land of the Ruthenians in Jotunheim and met with their King, to which a plan was created to woo the Jotun princess Rindr into

Gjallarhorn

procreative copulation with him. To this end Wotan disguised himself as two successive handsome Knechten (Knights). However, Princess Rindr denied the sexual advances of both forms that the Wanderer presented. He then cut and anointed runes to cause sickness in Rindr, and proceeded to disguise himself then as a medicine woman: a Völva, which is a form known to be assumed by Odin, and mentioned by Loki in the *Lokasenna*, being the events that directly proceeded this.

The Völva promised a cure for Rindr's ailments, though there was a negative side effect that he-as-she warned of, which was that of a violent reaction. Rindr nonetheless consented to the treatment, and the King under the orders of the disguised Terrible One, tied his daughter to the bed in bondage. Then the High God resumed his natural form, and proceeded to *violently rape* Rindr. The violence of the act impregnated her with a child of likewise pure, bloodthirsty violence. Rindr gave birth to Vali, who then

Gjallarhorn

grew to full adulthood in a single day, and directly sought out vengeance for his slain brother. Over time Rindr would be catalogued as one of the Ásynjur, which are the female Æsir. It follows that the producing of a child and the bloodline therefrom was enough to graft the Jotun princess into the vine of goddesses, as the Jotunar were often treated as chattel, and subjected to indignities manifold in all else-while occurrences. And this tale has the unique dual perspective of Rindr's status before and after the birth of Vali.

It is not uncommon within Germanic mythology for the Ases to regard the Jotunar as divine collateral. The Giants were in all senses "lesser beings," of which they would regularly exploit in all ways imaginable: financial, sacrificial, and in this case reproductive.

They were also sexually exploited, as recounted in the flyting poem *Harbarðsljod*. In the verse, Odin brags about his promiscuous conquests while traveling in Jotunheim, recalling his perversing of seven sisters all, seducing the Witch-wives of Jotunar away from them for his lust, and an altogether perseveration on his carnal wicked appetite.

Troubling here for many readers is a foreboding passage which Wotan recounts: *These women were wise to give themselves freely to me.* Suggesting something dark and transgressive in the wake of denial. As Odin's thirst for the womanly flesh, and his grim resolve to have the sex of theirs for his taking, is entirely unrivaled in all of comparative mythology. He wasn't just a god of sex, but also of sexual conquest, and the symbol of

Gjallarhorn

male virility driven to the dark extreme.

At this juncture, we will begin to examine this in its entirety, which is precisely the opposite of what traditionally occurs in the arenas most suitable for the discussion. Rather than reactionary accord, the Draugr Cult tends to place an analytic eye upon everything it is confronted with, moving away from the celebratory binaries of disgust and enthusiasm alike. For this is a dense topic before us. Furthermore it is challenging, and that is precisely what lies at the center of its malabsorption or malpractice.

Using our Wamphyric praxis, beginning at the most basic of interpretations, it is commonly understood that the skalds and historians of the ancient world recorded the mythos for various different reasons. In the beginning, it would be entirely standard for a skald to be crafting his poetry and mythos *as a reflection of nature*, and to this degree, few but pointed literary minds have interpreted the Rape of Rindr as the change from the winter season to that of the spring. In fact, all of Odin's consorts have been, seen through this lens (by several scores of individuals), as symbols of the Earth. In this manner, Frigg could be seen as the cultivated land, representing agriculture and the yielding of crops. Jord or Fjorgyn would be the untethered land, and producing wild foliage. Rindr in this view could be seen as the frozen land of winter, unwilling to yield to the breaking of its icy grip, unwilling to submit to the fertility of the vernal or spring equinox.

Another potentiality is that this story was the result of

Gjallarhorn

Christian Influence and specifically crafted as a *conversion tool*. This wouldn't be out of the realm of possibility, as the most complete version was recorded by Saxo Grammaticus in his seminal 13th century work *Gesta Danorum*. Being a Danish historian and theologian, notwithstanding the secretary to the Archbishop of Lund places the agenda of the legend recorded in this extensive detail under the shadow of suspicion.

Scandinavia was notoriously difficult to convert entirely to Christianity. Several manners of transition techniques were done through the ages. Such as the integration of Christ Jesus into the Pantheon of Nordic Gods. He was a Roman addition, whose throne and seat of power was located at the base of Yggdrasil by the Well of Urd, according to Snorri Sturluson in the Younger Edda. He also had his own afterlife called *Wind-Hall,* where the dead could abide eternity as heroic angels in his employ.

Another tactic, which would become the successful one was to mandate Christianity as the official, public faith, while permitting individuals to worship the old gods in private. This continued on for a very long time, and would give birth to magickal practices, stripped of their full origins and surviving in the use of staves and hex signs.

However, there is also the grim likelihood that a type of *black propaganda* was used by the church against the heathen faith. Whereas most of us do know *where* the codified mythology was emanating from, not everyone is aware. Germanic mythology by and large is assumed to have been written down via oral

Gjallarhorn

transmission, and for a large part, it was, but *who* was writing it down is a critical factor here: Christian Monks, Theologians and persons educated in clerical institutions. It's not *often* remembered or even spoken of, that this was the case. And yet it is factually accurate.

With so many people entrusted with the exegesis of this work failing to include or intentionally omitting this portion of its history opens the mythos to a vulnerability which threatens from beyond the threshold of its doorways into the outside realm.

What has been discussed hitherto is what the Draugr Cult calls *the Fireside Apprehension*, which includes the rational, and the symbolic, intended to provide an influential framework which can inform, empower and accelerate all corporeal thoughts and endeavors — removing the dramatic, the extreme, the mystic, and the fanciful. But this is not the only apprehension held by the Draugr Cult. There is also *the Shadowside Apprehension*, in which views many of these things not just as a pockets or waves of natural energy that would in other cases sub-atomically cause change in conformity with will. No, according to the *Shadowside Apprehension,* Odin is real.

And it would follow that with such a change in perspective, this tale really happened. Meaning, Odin violently raped a Jotun princess, and exulted in it. As he did in all matters of sexual lust. Here it would be astute to remember that while Odin violently raped the Jotun Princess Rindr, this was not an event that occurred between mortals. This legend recounts an interaction between mythic being and mythic being. Within the cosmological legend of Norse Mythology, it is recounted that Odin created the Earth, determined its laws and was the cosmic populater. Outside of the primordial realms of ice and fire, as well as the abyss, not much else lacked his authoring signature. That includes most of the worlds along the cosmic tree, their inhabitants, and all that is within.

Odin is the supreme personality of godhead. So when the intelligence behind the matrix of the Omni-verse decides upon something, it's going to happen. There are no two ways about that. Of course in Germanic Heathenism, the practice is then by proxy subject to the scrutiny that should but does not accompany many such divine acts of infallibility.

Because in the synoptic gospels, when the Lord God sent a message to announce that Mary would be receiving the holy seed through immaculate conception, there is no record of her agency of choice. The Lord God does what the Lord God does. To question that at some point meant execution, independent of its justification or otherwise.

For many years, the general population of Europe wasn't allowed to read the Bible. There was a concern that the holy writ synthesized in the hands of the common folk would be an abomination. Those without the clerical training necessarily would in theory not possess the proper frame of reference to process what was going on, in the Bible.

And it would follow that Mary, Mother of Jesus would be canonized thereafter as a figure to be venerated in Catholic prayer, meditation, and *living example*. She became a heavenly being, capable of intercession with earthly events to the degree that influence might come as a result of petition upon her behalf, though always and ultimately attributed to the almighty hand of her immortal and infallible rapist.

So too would Rindr be canonized, and in the single instance in the mythos where she is not a Jotun (a divine being already) and simply a human princess, she still received ascension into the ranks of the Ásynjur. Yet in Catholicism and its derivative denominations, this event is seen as beautiful, miraculous and *immaculate*. Even though, it was foretold to her by a terrifying celestial being, often bursting with electrum, with skin on fire

as if coming from a furnace. Mary, Mother of Jesus *didn't have agency* in that legend. She was told by a figure that scared her half to death, likely, as in the Old Testament, an encounter with an Enochian being was always met with madness, mortal terror and mental as well as physical paralysis.

Therefore, *it was violent*. And it was also coercive. Yet these matters are either forgotten or altered in favor of presentation or general political maintenance. In the case of Odin's rape of Rindr, the story is not whitewashed, or altered, or made to be told in a weaselly way. No, quite the opposite. It is raw and unmitigated, much like nature is. For there is no choice in when the winter gives way to the spring, no matter how much it clings to its new purity. Spring will come and the seeds of the new year will be laid without consent, by beings

Gjallarhorn

that are sentient and otherwise.

In a manner of rational discussion, we are now getting into the side of Paganism that is beautiful beyond compare, and also, very much historic in behavior. These myths existed for many reasons. Among them: early scientific understanding of the processes of the earth. Primal yes, in the sense that they were encoded and delivered in tales dressed in entertaining factors, but no less valuable, and especially for the time.

What we see when the dust of the discussion has settled is something critically ignored: careful analysis. It may be that the Germanic Paganism of the world in which we live in, and has developed into what it is today, is no longer equipped to digest these dark and morbid tales, extracting from them their value and function of which they originally served.

Which is why the Draugr Cult maintains a healthy distance from these terms: Heathenry, Paganism, and Odinism. To a degree.

We are all these things: yes, affirmative, ja. But in truth the terms no longer encapsulate what we are today, with the Draugar being both ancient and modern. Today we are Draugar, and it is an evolutional of all things, evolved adjacently and alongside those which informed it. It is this uniqueness that separates us from our stillborn counterparts and opens doorways still into the nine worlds.

Gjallarhorn

Fires of Wotan

When I was growing up, I had never heard even the most remote whisper of Odinism as a young man. I would have considered myself *very* well-read at the time, even in Medieval literature. To make matters worse I had access to the Internet, which by comparison looked and operated in our lives very differently than how it does now. With all of these things at my disposal, and the general push towards intrigue, one would normally presuppose that I would have organically stumbled upon it by myself- but it was not so. There were times when a situation

Gjallarhorn

or setting would allow the astral forces to onset in great amounts, and in hindsight I can see that there was always a link back to the Germanic Antiquity for when this was concerned.

When I did finally discover and then immerse myself in this universe, I was very surprised that, the remnants of this subject were largely nowhere to be found in our everyday culture, language and in the spirit of the age — not consciously. Yes people were aware of Paganism, and the occult, but *Germanic* esotericism and *Germanic* belief were equally alienic concepts — to many. The absence within even academia was alarming. I had a medieval studies professor, who eventually became my student advisor, and it turned out that he was just as intrigued with this subject as I was. However,

we were both equally "in the dark" about it.

If I had the desire to discuss this with anyone on the outside of some involvement or another, the response was always the same: *this sounds like you made it up.* If they only knew how *incorrect* they actually were. And of course if you were to seek out those Germanic gurus where they could be found: *fraudsters, one and all.* Most who were interested in this subject *then* very clearly had a vested interest in why they had attached themselves to its spirit. Of course as a young man, with priorities, it was hard to meet *everyone,* and determine through assessment whether they were a credible source or otherwise. In fact, the reality is that there *were* credible sources. Mostly in the fringe societies they were: National Socialist Black Metal, Neofolk,

Gjallarhorn

Skinhead Culture and various Racial Societies of the time. You also had a *few* laudable groups, such as *The Odinic Rite* from the UK, and the Asatru Folk Assembly from Vinland. Though these too would both in time join the ranks of those deemed *undesirable* to the modern world: labeled then as white supremacy and hate groups.

You see, in the quest to distance their religion from everything they personally disagreed with on the political spectrum, Unversalist Asatru have sacrificed authenticity in its wake, especially in writ as well as in deed. For, to pick up any volume penned by one of their tree hierophants reveals something of a tragedy — that so much is to be lost, when one fights against nature.

I know plenty of folk who are racially conscious, and don't live their lives driven by politically directed agendas. It doesn't have to be that way. And yet Odinism in many ways can't and won't be divorced from its racial makeup, because *that* is a key focus of the mysteries of the north. It is that our blood is connected to the ancient ancestors that the Eddas tell of. That our blood is magickal. And we alone possess the same potential as the progenitors of the divine lineage.

So much of what this is made of, is *just not for the masses*, and that is something that I learned growing up. It was *a hard lesson*, finding myself as a social pariah, in every possible scenario, because I wore my ancestral beliefs on my sleeve. Because I let it guide my life and its choices, and I spoke about that *openly*.

Don't do this.

Gjallarhorn

This is not the way our ancestors had planned for us to operate in times like these. And this goes further to say that there is a time and place for everything. Maybe in the distant future there will be a time when we can openly gather, discuss and make a physical presence for ourselves among the general populace.

There are signs that this time might be approaching. When the History Channel released their television powerhouse competitor, *Vikings*, to the reborn syndication franchise world, going toe-to-toe with programs like *The Walking Dead*, and then *proving* the popularity of the subject regarding the ancient Germanic past, its customs and its beliefs, a turning point occurred in our time as it concerns Odinism.

It became popular. It became en vogue. It "woke up," like many things tend to after a time of dormancy.

The Draugr Cult operates in secrecy. We don't want to be making our ways and our customs displayed out in the open attached to our Fireside personalities — not right now. Therefore it behooves us to regularly practice a method of esoteric detachment from the finer points of our ways *when they are not being used,* for several reasons. For to operate in such a manner will signal your immediate sequestering into an area of limited stroke. There is a value in secrecy that one begins to fully comprehend when studying *how* Odinism has survived through the fires of the burning times. That is: a private manner. Many people tend to do this, but only the Draugr Cult has mastered it, and like all roles one assumes, you can not simply *adopt* something for "show" — you *must* immerse into it. You *must* become it, when needed. *SHADOWS OVER GERMANIA* goes into this concept, and here we examine it in close detail as to allow *you* the reader to exercise perfect delivery of this extremely effective esoteric technique of changing apprehensions.

There is a systemic issue within the realm of Paganism, and all esotericism for that matter. It is the inability to withstand the seduction of the Shadowside. In this apprehension, all manner of mythic emanation is understood as real and accessible. In the Shadowside, there is no metaphor, no symbolism, only palpable forces separated by the enigma that is the veil between our world and the next. This perspective — this view — is necessary for any/ all magickal operation to be executed with skill, and to be effective, let alone effect at all. However, two major pitfalls exist for the esotericist approaching the Shadowside: its timely approach in learning / experience, and its timely arrest. If for no other reason, the polarities of the Fireside and the Shadowside simply cannot exist without one another, in any sense of the idea, within the experience of the finite life of the host body vessel of the undead.

Too much time in the Shadowside will deteriorate anyone. We are simply not equipped to operate in terms of the mystic in overwhelming patterns. Furthermore, existing merely as a esoteric mind not only courts dangerous inertia, but it also garners a lowly reputation among peers, whose compliance and admiration you *should* strive to capture. As it is

Gjallarhorn

Gjallarhorn

simply unreasonable and in all areas *lacking strategy* to succumb to the life of a witless worm.

One may adopt the archetype of the *outsider*, but such things become old very quickly, when certain marks of success *in the real world* are missed, lost or ruined. Therefore this article will regard methods in stoking the flames of the Fireside.

Most unseasoned neonates have to instigate the Shadowside, since they are still in the early stages of experiencing the reality of the Undead, the Astral and the forces of darkness. By contrast, the sorcerer whether by physis or breeding must take heed to perform continual instigation of the Fireside, in order to balance the plummeting depths of the Ginnungagap.

Let us consider the alternative to the Shadowside. It would be something entirely symbolic, psychological and scientific. While the Fireside has room for belief in the forces beyond, it regards them as unnecessary of deep meditation. The Fireside Wamphyr arises from their slumber and seeks out necessities that assist to build or maintain the path of harsh alchemical development and vice versa. The Fireside Wamphyr has no thoughts about God or Gods, or customs or traditions. No, the Fireside is about the essentials. It is far removed from indwelling the blood of Wotan, and more centered in experiencing the modalities of yourself, and not the figure of Odin — at least not the Shadowside Odin.

For the Fireside Odin is merely a symbol of Nature.

Gjallarhorn

This includes nature as a phenomenon, nature as an organic hyper-being with its own biospheric intelligence, as well as the nature of *yourself*. These subjects are often buried deeply under the polemics of unicellular persons who also have barely a cursory understanding of the ancestral heathen weltanschauung from which they derive 100% of their identity.

This is an exercising in discovery, in personal upkeep, and the exploration of personal meaning within the finite lifespan of the mortal vessel.

While there is no set formula for this extended magickal working, the following synopsis can serve to abbreviate its nature for guidance purposes.

Begin on a new day, and try your best to regiment these techniques with transitions such as this. Upon waking, strike and continually strike all thoughts about esoteric matters. In the Fireside apprehension, they are not welcome — not right now. Valhalla is a symbol, it deserves no serious mental energy to contemplate over it. Wotan is life giving air that your breathe on the brisk spring morning, but also the claw that tore the prey asunder near your garden — being ever mindful of what *nature* really means.

He is not a bearded elder enthroned in a celestial hall, nor a physical wanderer of curious penchant. Though, these and all forms are ones that this force may assume or, more so, possess. Only in a single and specific apprehension, that of the Shadowside mind, is the Allfather an anthropomorphic being. In the others, such as the Fireside and the mysterious Götterdämmerung — that

Gjallarhorn

latter which we seek to walk between the worlds in esoteric mastery, understands this entity as related wholly (in the first) and part (in the latter) *an energy*, and a *matrix* for which this energy exists in a state of flux. To connect with it, is to *link into* that vast and astral *computer* which governs the mechanism of *all-things*.

It has no gender, hair or eye color, physical makeup or even set characteristics. If anything, it is all possibilities, and in this, nothing definite at all.

And yet it is the celestial, astral blood possessed by the Germani which serves as the *password or security clearance* that grants access to it.

These are useful things for you. They offer a valuable symbolic framework for which metaphor helps to file a basic understanding of the physical constituents of practical reality. Furthermore, in their lack of existence, you capitalize on the opportunity to embody the closest thing in reality that they might be.

The concepts of things like fate and alchemy are paralyzed and cannot be rationally approached — not now. That is beneath you. Right now, you are focused simply on *what you want,* but furthermore, *what you need.* Start with the latter, and work your way backwards. You need food and hydration: focus on that. You need to ready yourself for the day: focus on that too. You need meaningful interpersonal communication and interaction: focus, focus, focus. You need money — all roads lead to focus.

Gjallarhorn

Bog Blades: The Uncanny History of the Norse - Gaels

If you were to ask someone in a learning institution today: "Were the Celts also Vikings?" then the answer you would receive would unilaterally be a lie. Such a lie is not just commonly understood as fact, but it is also hardwired into the mentality of those from the United Kingdom and the British Isles. In fact, the lie is widespread across the globe, in every country, and in every institution, with the truth being buried under layers of historical darkness.

Let us begin with saying that Icelanders, those envisioned as the

Gjallarhorn

torchbearers of Norse Mythology, and continued privatized custom, are genetically 50% Celtic with a standard deviation based on what chromosome is being examined. But how is this so?

Originally Iceland was colonized *majorly* by the inhabitants of Orkney, Shetland, the Hebrides, the Isle of Islay, the Isle of Man and Northern Ireland. These are all peripheries of Scotland following the Norwegian invasions of the Viking Era. These lands were conquered and then ruled for many centuries until the ultimate absorption of these areas into the land it is now called, minus the Isle of Man and Northern Ireland. When Iceland was first discovered, there was some minor evidence of Christian priesthood being present beforehand, but not much. The primary settlers came from the Nornish lands.

Norn: the language of the Northmost Scots, which are generations upon generations of a Norse-Gael admixture. Because the Norwegians did not just settle and rule the periphery of Scotland, but also intermarried with the Gaelic populace.

Could you blame them?

If not the hereditary Norn, then the Norns carried with them the Gaelic slaves under their yoke, to the newly discovered Iceland, and therefore we have, what is known today as Icelanders: roughly half Norse, roughly half Gaelic. And here is where it gets *very* interesting, in that Iceland would become the place in which the most cherished of Norse Mythology would be codified. Could we have known under these layers of forgetfulness and deliberate obfuscation, that Snorri Sturluson was half-Celt?

34

Gjallarhorn

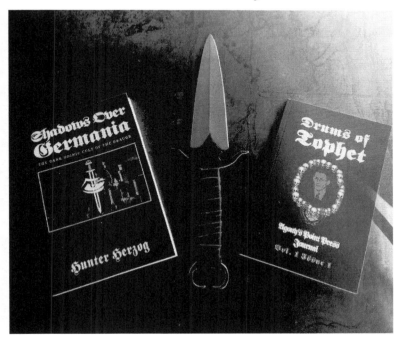

The answer is a hard: No.

Because Celticism means something very important to the areas of the UK that are not largely dominated by the rule of the crown. Brythonic folk are heavily concentrated in Wales, and Ireland for a large part, but not in the UK and not in Scotland.

The latter for instance has two major Germanic hyper-bloodlines flanking, first from the Anglo-Saxon Lowlanders, and then the Nornish Highlanders coupled with the Nornish Islanders. Celticism in Scotland is more of a romantic idea: something of a uniqueness of identity that coincided with the recession of Viking and Saxon rule.

Scottish DNA for instance is very intriguing. It is found all over Norway, the Faroe Islands, and Iceland, for which it is far stronger connected to than anywhere truly Brythonic, like Wales or the majority of Ireland. Anywhere in Scotland for that matter, be it the center of the mainland or spanning outward in any direction becomes increasingly Germanic wherever you go.

Even more interesting is the level of which Odinism has been hidebound or forever branded into the spirit of Scotland. Notwithstanding many areas still bear his name: such as Odinsgarth, Otterswick and Odin Bay. And there are more...

The Standing Stones of Stenness is a Neolithic site in Orkney which existed long before the arrival of the Norse, but eventually became a place in which the Vikings imprinted their esoteric beliefs and practices. Referring back to the DNA comparison between the Scottish and the Icelanders, it makes perfect sense that before Scottish unification in 1418, they evidentially held the same Icelandic custom of maintaining a public affiliation with the church, while privately permitting the veneration of the old gods. Such as the Odin Stone in Stenness, used until the 1700's for secret Odinic worship, until its ultimate felling within the century's span.

However, following the birth of the new country would also bring with it a new (adopted) identity, and also, new customs to outmode the old. With these customs came the rescinding of the Nornish practice of private heathen worship. Though, many practices still hailed from

Gjallarhorn

the old world of the North and took root in Scotland. Solingen steel from Germany, and their smithing techniques were adopted over time in the forging of "holy weapons," particularly of the dagger type, for which oaths would be sworn upon. These would develop into many models, such as the ballock, a popular item also used widely in the Scandinavias, and "bog blades" such as the dirk and the sgian dubh, which are both descendants of the ballock, as is the Scottish naval dagger.

The attitude they applied to this example of ceremonial *and* sidearm tool was purely scalped from the Pagan customs of old. The Solingen steel and German smithery were used due to the technique's ability to forge steel that could *command, attract and direct spirits*. The custom of swearing oaths upon these specific blades is a significant indicator of eldern custom as well. It was as if these daggers held a type of link to their soul. And the soul of the Scotsman is undisputedly pagan.

And it should be so, this mystic relationship to their weaponry, given their comparative behavior towards them. As the bog blade was the katana of the Scottish, for which they would never leave it away from them for too long. With a vast majority of Scotland being financially destitute, a proper sword was often not something reasonably affordable, so the bog blade became the most popular alternative. They were symbols of espionage, all of which points back to Odin, with many of these being *concealable blades* as they would be drawn and used quickly, unannounced and by the time that it was too late. Looking at the design, one can't help but notice the cræft of what can otherwise be called nothing else then *a spear point knife* that while has a handle, also lacks a hand guard. It looks like a spear point, which can be mounted. There are some designs even today that *look as if* they are intended to be placed at the head of a pole arm and thrust at an enemy. Again this all speaks to the condition of extreme poverty for which the Scots found themselves in. One blade becomes many things: and that is Odinic.

Soon after in 1421, legend began to speak of "the Shrouded One of Odin" who was a widow with three children, who had been discovered by a priest while in the middle of her pagan rites. Tradition states that the priest offered to spare her life if she offered her body in sexual union to him, but it is also stated that she denied this bargain. It is said that the priest then rallied a mob who then executed her: first by pulling out her eyes, then her tongue with hot irons, and after her body was brutally beaten (and likely raped — repeatedly) they took her, quivering, to a mound of slow burning wood, and set her aflame to die slowly. This all before her children to bear witness.

Her three children, two boys and a girl, were then offered a new bargain: convert to Christianity, or suffer the same, perhaps worse. They agreed, at least as a ruse. One year following their mother's execution, they returned to her grave that was customary to dishonour among the townsfolk with urine, feces, cum and all manner of filth. Rather than a libation of heinous offense, they poured blood upon the soil, in the tradition of the old way.

Gjallarhorn

It is told that their mother then appeared as an apparition, and instructed all three children to become the genesis of a clandestine conspiracy: a secret "Brotherhood of Odin," for which the group would then be called.

As far back as can be attested by oral tradition, this tale has been told at least since the 1970's, mostly within magickal orders, but it was in the early 1990's that a doctoral student at the university of Glasgow wound assert and confirm contact made with the Brotherhood of Odin, and in 1992, the seminal work by the same name would be published, regarded as non-fiction by even the publishers.

In the ensuing years a heightened interest would bloom in regards to the Brotherhood of Odin, and Asatruar Kindreds began to suspect, as is claimed in the aforementioned book, that once Norse Heathenry began to legally organize and meet en masse, the Brotherhood of Odin made it an imperative to send *at the very least*, one representative to each Kindred or Coven, even for a time, just to see "what was going on, in there."

What is truly surprising is that the Brotherhood has both the wisdom and highly developed system to back up their claims. Practicing necromancy, blood rites, sacrifice and attempting to create rifts in the space-time continuum in order to travel to "other worlds."

The Odin Brotherhood boasts of advantageous operations of their adepts, in such a manner in which they have and continue to physically confront the Gods on their own familiar planes of regular existence. There is a tale of a man who journeyed through time and

Gjallarhorn

space to Valhalla, and spoke with the Einherjar who were in the middle of their nightly feast of pork and ale. He mocked the Gods when he saw them, and they threatened him, to which he then informed them that he feared neither god nor man. In this display of courage, they all bellowed in welcoming laughter and bid him to join them in their feast as a brother and friend. Unfortunately he could not stay and returned to the world of men.

It is difficult to discern whether what is being described in the work is a physical group of individuals or a "spiritual ideal" in which anyone who is "called" might join. Within the text, there is argument that can be found for both. What remains significant about the Odin Brotherhood is its inspiring legend of Odinism in the UK, and also with many shared customs presenting within the Draugr Cult.

Gjallarhorn

The Eye of Grimnir

Within and without of ceremony, the voice of the orator is reached out and twines with the strands of the astral plane, encoding with the language many unspoken directives that cannot be detected by the untrained recipient. Despite being a deity of war, Odin rarely engaged in it himself. In the mythos, it is abundantly clear that he as a being appreciated the finer elements of conflict: that which occurs at the subatomic level. There is an entire hermetic dimension associated with our interactions in all things: those physical, spiritual and otherwise. This realm is ruled by the phenomenon of character, charisma and witticism, and while these things may seem to be inborn, to some, these skills can be dissected, hotwired, harnessed and programmed in individuals so choosing.

For it must be recognized that even inside of ceremonial magick, that without these skills, not much can be hoped for. The Undead can detect a weak soul, far quicker than one could even realize it within. Therefore it behooves the operator to hone in on these subjects for immediate development, and ultimate utilization.

Commanding the forces of darkness, is the same as commanding a person in the flesh. We can even see the shades of these sciences redolent in the arts of the ancient world. As Odin was a god of poetry, so too do these skills make their appearances in the nature of how this art is delivered. English poetry for instance when written in proper form takes on metric units intended to be read but also spoken. There is iambic pentameter, which is the standard form of an English Sonnet. Each line includes ten syllabic upward and downward inflections, or an unstressed syllable followed by a stressed one, always landing on the latter. That pattern is called an *iamb,* which is a type of poetic meter, with each meter (also called a "foot" or "feet" for plural use) comprised of two of these inflections or unstressed/ stressed syllables. When these feet are used in repetition, it is called "rhythm" and thus Iambic Pentameter. There is also Iambic Tetrameter and Iambic Trimeter.

The poetry of the ancient Germani is most often remembered in the Skaldic form, emanating from Iceland, for a large part. But it is also important to remember that the English language is also a Germanic one. Its poetry: just as auspicious. Unlike prose which is sometimes long winded by comparison, poetry is meticulously crafted, with each word chosen deliberately for a specific function. The craft of the stanza: an art. With each meter ending on a downward inflection, and thus an iamb, this ensures that these words, one and all, crawled through in coupled-syllables, *land,* in a way that the listener receives them in a pointed, remembered fashion.

That is the nature of the downward inflection. It carries with it the audial telegraph of confidence, surety and knowledge. A downward inflection begins and ends with a single syllable. In the beginning, the tone drops downward signaling a conclusion of the cadence or the rhythm, and ends with an finite, definite stop. Rather than the hit of a gavel, it is more of a drop, "finishing" the statement. There are many statements made in our everyday interactions that are *not* finished. Many people have no pointed or artistic rhythm of communication, and if the downward inflection of poetic speech is to be utilized, isolated, as a form of *mind control*, then it must be practiced if not already present.

As a science, this study is part of a larger discipline called *neuro-linguistic programming*, and it is very much the practice of *neuromancy*, insomuch as the manner of how one communicates to another, as well as to oneself, produces change in conformity with will. NLP may be relegated to pseudoscience, and especially so in the lands of the far north where the psychological field is *far more advanced* than that of virtually anywhere else on

Gjallarhorn

the planet, but it serves to investigate in terms of trial, error, effectiveness and otherwise. NLP asserts that there is an intrinsic link between communication and behavior, but even furthermore, behavioral-response. Using the model of NLP, which also uses its theory to dissect potential cosmological models such as the kabbalistic tree of life, and such as the tree of Yggdrasil, this will be heavily featured in the next Draugr Cult book titled *NORN: The High Magick of Draugrism*. In this approach, a single psychological model can be graphed using modalities and sub-modalities, and these translate in occult terms to things like Sephiroth and the attributes of the Sephiroth, but according to NLP we each have our own personal tree of modalities which cements across the journey through experiences. One can examine the personal tree

using methods of NLP but also examine someone else and discover their own personal occult profile.

One can effectively do this within analysis following the behavior response to the downward inflection and its acquiescence to command, displayed across a wide range of expertise mental statements. One does this by altering the nature of the rhythm, the nature of the meter and the specific choice of downward inflections. Ending every sentence with a downward inflection will make you sound like a concentration camp robot, and the recipient or subject will likely detect that something is altogether *off* about the conversation. They will likely disengage the operator, and you want to avoid that if possible. Selecting *which* statements will *land* becomes something that can be mastered and determined *in*

Gjallarhorn

real time only micro-seconds before the verbal Mjölnir falls upon the skull of the Jotun.

To accent this concept, let's look at the follow statement.

"Satanic Front made me do it."

Now, let's review all possible downward inflections.

SATANIC FRONT made me do it.
Satanic Front MADE me do it.
Satanic Front made ME do it.
Satanic Front made me DO it.
Satanic Front made me do IT.

Mind control works precisely in this fashion, in that the synapses are formed by the professional within the brain of the subject which respond to the operator and their machinations. These experiential mechanisms solidify because they are mentally paired with events that are stressed, events that are downwardly inflected in the sense that an abrupt cessation of control is realized, and submission occurs. This can also be done simply with verbal interaction, making a subatomic mind control conditioning possible. What the subject does not know when NLP is being utilized, is that their minds are receiving a subtle battery of which loss of control is assumed. Shock is the catalyst bridges realization to submission and then ultimate programming. Which is why when a person is being verbally brainwashed in real time, the operator will likely choose targeted phrases based upon the subject's modalities (and the associated profile created), and downwardly inflect words or concluding words

Gjallarhorn

to empower an entire phrase that delivers shock. When shock is delivered, the brain becomes profoundly suggestible, since most of the subject's general mindset is in current suspension. Then, when the operator detects submission (which is the most suggestible state), a command can be given, or a mechanism for command — which is an entirely new modality altogether — can be constructed. Yes, you can create new Sephiroth in a person, using this method. Those modalities will have their own sub-modalities which include the seasons they were forged in, the weather and the scents in the room in which the operator may have deliberately planted. The colors featured in the environment, as well as the plants, symbols, food present and music playing all become the ingredients which can esoterically activate the modalities and their power.

Gjallarhorn

Gjallarhorn

Odinic Killer Rite: An Introduction to High Magick

It is believed that when a heinous and foul deed is performed, such as the taking of human life, that the environment and natural mechanism of organic reaction that occurs, between contact , heightened senses and all that is between born from the act itself, primes an unconscious and unknowing Wamphyric drinking of the lifeforce and

Gjallarhorn

the soul of the victims. These intelligences are then stored in the body of the assailant without direct realization of what has occurred, and over time, the torment of these spirits grows to terrible proportions. Never knowing what exactly has occurred, the killer progressively becomes more engulfed by the personal madness and pain of the victim(s).

Generally speaking in Wamphyrism, the lifeforce of a target is pulled psychically without any contact physical or otherwise with the individual, to which the Wamphyr then offers the lifeforce to the Undead in ceremony. The lifeforce does not stay inside of the body of the Wamphyr; such matters are either known inherently, passed along orally, or learned in the field. Lifeforce that stays in the Wamphyr has a tendency to expire in terms

of nourishment, and will begin to poison the creature if not moved in a time sensitive manner.

Therefore when someone who is not a Wamphyr, like a physical killer, accidentally happens upon the absorption of lifeforce in wholesale with a complete expiration of the target, we are indeed looking at *a lot* of lifeforce. If the killer has multiple victims, the intensity of the absorption, in theory, is manifold.

A Wamphyr who comprehends the nature of these things, *and* who is in a position to experience this phenomenon in the physical dayside world, such as an infantryman or a police officer, would understand that once that mechanism has occurred, usually as an unconscious result of a highly stressful environment, accessing many such acuities as a natural response, then at

Gjallarhorn

some point the Wamphyr would have to move that lifeforce to the Undead Gods, otherwise they would be consciously courting disaster.

The physical killer does not know this, and they often tend to spend many years incarcerated, with only the victims to keep his or herself company. The tortured souls magnify all things inside, corrupting what may have been to the killer as an unknown nectar, to that of a corrosive chemical or a toxin. The mind and the spirit of the killer deteriorate, and a type of natural justice occurs leaving the individual in question as a twisted, insane, basket case, babbling obscenities laced with occult truths, probably communicated to them *by the victims* in their retribution.

Such can be observed with Charles Manson.

As it regards Odinists, there have been in recent times many such persons of the mantle that have taken human life, and are currently still living. Some are incarcerated, and others are not any longer. Sometimes these individuals were politically driven, and aimed for the most numeric in terms of fatalities. Usually because they are politically motivated and in terrorism, numbers are what terrorists aim for. In other instances, Odinic killers are acting upon something born from an internal drive towards honor, or whatever they believe to merit their decision to commit the act of killing. Sometimes it has nothing to do with either of these things, and has no explanation; at least not one that can be discerned by investigation. Sometimes the individuals are Odinists before they've killed, and sometimes they convert after, while in prison. This

Gjallarhorn

latter category describes a lot of Odinic killers. One thing seems to unite them all: they dedicate their slayings to Odin, at some point, but lack the ability to transfer the souls to him.

Wamphyri are terrible deceivers, amoral bastards by trade, and are known to swindle their way through life, as a matter of tradecraft. For if the strong rule the weak, then the clever rule the strong — a maxim known to all Wamphyri.

Cleverness is a strength beyond strength, and it describes a faculty that sets the bar higher than brawn. If there is a might that is right, it is intelligence. Wotan is an archetype that represented this very specific situation, preferring to outwit, outsmart and outthink his opponents, with the exception of only two instances, being the creation and destruction

myths, and it is not known *how* Wotan advanced against Ymir, or how he will advance against the Fenris wolf at Ragnarok.

In all things, the Wamphyr operates at a level far beyond and above the generally positioned "occultist." That term in reality can not be compared to the harsh alchemical praxis that is Wamphyrism, as it is a marker of species. Notwithstanding, Wamphyrism has its own methods of magick, and those sorceries are often "occulted" as to avoid casting pearls before swine.

Our strain of Wamphyrism is called Draugrism, and it is denoted as such because it relates to a specific bloodline within the blood family of Wamphyrism — at least, the Draugrism that they are in contact with. For this praxis and this species claim a pedigree that stretches back into the nobilities of the Iron Age and potentially before. The Draugar that made contact with and were absorbed into the blood family did not *invent* it, only carried it over and fomented therewith a unique and demarcated bloodline of Teutonic Wamphyri. Those that form the Draugr Cult today present a synthesis of Sinister Wamphyrism and Wotanic Heathenry. They are unique, boisterous, macho, and delight in holy violence.

The Draugar are Warriors, in every sense of the meaning, but what separates them from the would-be chattel of the occult milieu, Asatru/ Odinism included, is that the Draugar are *acutely aware* that we live in modern times, largely removed from the distant past, and its normative customs. As the undead sentinels of Walvater-Wotan, they are ever ready to drink the lifeforce from the unsuspecting victims, often using techniques that can otherwise not be attributed in any legal sense to the operator. Within their scope and esoteric philosophy, there is a unique perseveration on the nature and practice of sacrifice to the Undead. It doesn't matter *who did the deed*, but what matters rather, is who is performing the sacrifice.

To this end the Odinic Killer Rite is an act of high sacrifice, and also, horrendous capitalization. Whereas the Draugar *that we know of* tend to avoid the pitfalls of criminal behavior, to a reasonable extent, that does not mean that the Draugar are not inimical and bloodthirsty workers of evil.

If the souls of the slain are trapped in the flesh of the murderer, then those souls can be *stolen* by the

Gjallarhorn

Draugar, and then sacrificed to the Undead Gods.

That the killer is, was or became an Odinist forges the astral link to which makes this rite applicable in the first place. And whereas this rite may be used to steal the souls inhabiting other types of killers, the likelihood of effect here is much greater. Also, with such a plethora of murderers who are Odinists, there is likely no end any time soon to the wellspring of lifeforce to be seized, especially when one considers that conversion to Odinism is a commonplace occurrence in the prison systems around the globe and therefore exist many Odinic killers that we would never know about, unless a case by case examination were to occur.

To perform the Odinic Killer Rite, assemble all of the tools already covered in the esoteric chapters of *Shadows Over Germania,* with the additional item of one that can establish a symbiotic link with the killer. In Draugrism, the nature of *contact* is stressed, because without such an occurrence, and without the following overlap of beings necessary to prime the moment for effective lifeforce feeding, no such methods will work. What we are referring to here specifically can manifest in the form of a photograph of the killer, or a bindrune which is charged with heavy personal lifeforce and that is laced with the thoughts, reflections, visualizations and energy emerged from the contemplation and/ or meditation on the killer. Or both. Or more things similar.

Perform the opening rite as described in the *Blood Magick* section of *Shadows Over Germania*. Once this

Gjallarhorn

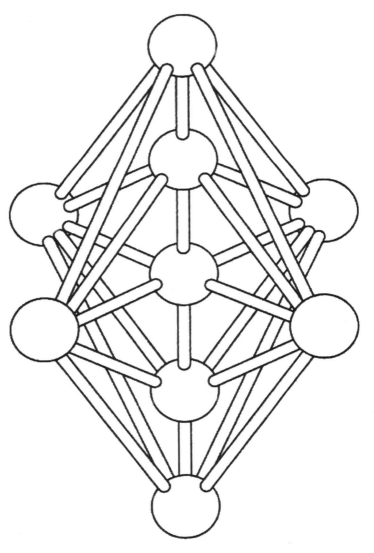

Gjallarhorn

is complete, using the planet that rules the astrological sign of the killer, summon the sphere associated. Note also that this will have to be performed *during the ruling hour of that planet.*

After the preliminary rite is performed in the center of the area of working, cast a sunwheel (parlance for a circular fylfot) upon a parchment, in either a specially prepared celestial elixir according to the western esoteric tradition, or a simple ink, or paint. Atop the center of the sunwheel place an additional smaller parchment with the planetary sigil necessary to make contact with the target's astrological sign. The Draugr can anoint this entire hyper-rune in blood, or imbue it with lifeforce according to the techniques of psychic wamphyrism. If possible place a photograph or another implement that

has had direct contact with the target, thus assisting the creation of the tunnel with which to achieve the ancient practice of sympathetic contact. The name of the planet in old Norse should then be called nine times. For each of the planets the formula here is given:

Saturn: *Asgardr*
Sol: *Ljosalfheimr*
Jupiter: *Nifelheimr*
Mars: *Jotunheimr*
Earth: *Midgardr*
Venus: *Vanaheimr*
Mercury: *Muspelheimr*
Luna: *Dokkalfheimr*
Neptune: *Helheimr*

Uranus: *Ginnungagap*

Note: only seven of these spheres rule the zodiac. The others are provided for readers desiring to practice advanced Draugr High Magick on their own.

Once this has been done, the Draugr then with the ceremonial knife, casts the astrological sign of the target into the air hovering over the hyper-rune. When this is done, the Draugr then calls the full name of the target nine times. Now the astral simulacrum has been forged in full. The Draugr may then, from above, reach through the astrological sign that was cast, being the gateway to the target, and touch the parchment, or the photograph atop the parchments, completing the stages first of contact and then of penetration.

The methods of feeding are covered in *Shadows Over Germania*, and these guides should be followed. Drain the target of psychic lifeforce, first with nine breaths of inward pull indwelling lifeforce, and after the ninth repetition, call out the name of the killer's victim. Continue the process of drinking lifeforce from the target. Repeat the nine breaths inward, and the utterance of the victim's name, until you can detect that the victim's soul has been completely stolen. If there are more than one victims that the killer has claimed, move on to the next and repeat the process. Continue as desired, with the knowledge that the entire larceny does not need to be completed in a single rite.

As a cautionary note, these are the souls of the murdered dead. They are entities that have likely grown to unsustainable proportions of malignancy. It is not wise to wait long before the sacrifice to Walvater-Wotan and the Einherjar is made. The vengeful dead will wreak havoc upon their new prison, so take heed to be swift in the offering to the Terrible One. The methods of sacrifice are discussed in *Shadows Over Germania*, and can be used to immediately transfer the

Gjallarhorn

essence of the dead, to the abysmal goblet of the Allfather.

In my experience and rites as Draugr, it has been observed that even the smallest amount of sacrifice to the ravengod will produce the maximum effect. For while evil beyond limitation, the gifts of Wotan are black and baleful, carrying with them excesses and blasphemies with which no follower of White Krist could behold without feeling their puritanical soul trampled by the violence of eight hooves.

And this regards the nature of minimal, low sacrifices.

Imagine then what might be granted for such a great and terrible offering of evil!

Gjallarhorn

more from

Gjallarhorn

Agony's Point Press

Gjallarhorn

Gjallarhorn

As vultures turn counter-clockwise in the sky, as evil planets appear in the firmament and the anchors among the celestial bodies reverse their orbit – as blood and human body parts rain down from starships emanating from the subterranean heavenly planets, the planets of the ghosts and the hellish planets themselves, so extinguishing the sacrificial fires of the sages, by all these signs you will know that we are approaching. The undead - the monarchs inhabiting the despotic helm of the Court of Ahaz – the evil kings and queens of old, the warriors of renown. In days of yore we were known as the Rephaim but now we possess the bodies of those administering this wamphyric house –

three-hundred and thirty-three evil spirits to one possessed, undead uncaring "walking death" flesh-body wamphyr – often more. Those who seek human identity in such entombed fleshly vessels do so in error for it is only us so inhabiting – wave upon wave, rank upon rank. We issue this dark summons only to those who genuinely resonate with the inhumane – those who lust with black, fanatical will to hold aloft accursed swords of total death – recreating this earth as cemetery. Dark stars call, shadow planets leverage their hideous grasp obsessing, possessing. Our black hand is upon you. Cross the barrier, step through the passage, embrace that hitherto forbidden. Immortality awaits in world aflame.

Gjallarhorn

Gjallarhorn

In the Valley of Hinnom, the ancient residing place of the Rephaite, the drums of Tophet were beaten to drown out the sounds of screaming from the children being sacrificed to Moloch. As the funerary smoke of a world aflame chokes the globe those drums beat once again. Walk with us through the fire.

Gjallarhorn

Shadows Over Germania

THE DARK ODINIC CULT OF THE DRAUGR

Hunter Herzog

Gjallarhorn

Presenting the first esoteric work on Draugrism, Shadows Over Germania soars on raven's wings through the legends of the ancient and modern clandestine cult of the Teutonic Wamphyri. As the Undead sentinels of Walvater Wotan, the Draugar are possessed by hostile intelligences under the employ of the Wild Hunt. A tome of primal Blood Magick, of Odinism, of Viking Religion and the cutting edge of modern Wamphyrism. Shadows Over Germania strikes as the intense, blood-poem of Oden; a wolven grimoire for those who thirst to indwell the blood of the Eternal Hunter. Swords drawn in shadows, the Draugar rise in brutal winter.

Made in the USA
Monee, IL
02 April 2024

56243568R00039